611 Ways to Do More in a Day

611 Ways to Do More in a Day

Stephanie Culp

BETTERWAY BOOKS
CINCINNATI, OHIO

611 Ways to Do More in a Day. Copyright © 1998 by Stephanie Culp. Manufactured in the United States. All rights reserved. No part of this book may be reproduced in any form or by any electronic or mechanical means including information storage and retrieval systems without permission in writing from the publisher, except by a reviewer, who may quote brief passages in a review. Published by Betterway Books, an imprint of F&W Publications, Inc., 1507 Dana Avenue, Cincinnati, Ohio 45207. (800) 289-0963. First edition.

Other fine Betterway Books are available from your local bookstore or direct from the publisher.

02   01   00   99   98   5   4   3   2   1

Library of Congress Cataloging-in-Publication Data

Culp, Stephanie
    611 ways to do more in a day / Stephanie Culp.
      p.   cm.
    ISBN 1-55870-475-2 (pbk.: alk. paper)
    1. Time management—Miscellanea. 2. Home economics—Miscellanea. I. Title. II. Title: Six hundred and ten ways to keep your day from slipping away. III. Six hundred ten ways to keep your day from slipping away.
HD69.T54C847   1998
640'.43—DC21   98-10401
                                          CIP

Edited by Julie Wesling Whaley
Production Edited by Michelle Kramer
Interior designed by Daniel Pessel
Cover designed by Candace Haught

This book is dedicated to Diane Johnson in
Oconomowoc, Wisconsin.

Thank you for contributing your shining work ethic, your
conscientious intelligence, and your patient friendship to this,
and other books. You really are the best.

Acknowledgments

I sometimes think a book will write itself. Of course that never happens. This book started where all my books start—with the respected Mert Ransdell. Along the way a few other people had the nerve to work with me and provide significant contributions, including Diane Johnson, Dave Borcherding and Michelle Kramer. And when all is said and done, I am confident that the always important Hugh Gildea will be there to bring the book happily to the complete circle that I have grown accustomed to. High fives to everybody, including Boca and Bum for this, my ninth book.

Table of Contents

4 **Getting Things Done** 48

---

5 Finding Time for You and Yours 101

Introduction

How was your day yesterday? What about today and tomorrow? Do you get out of bed in the morning and hit the floor running, only to fall into bed at night too exhausted to figure out how the day got away from you? Has your To Do list taken over your life, leaving you no time for yourself?

With today's hectic pace and lifestyle choices, getting through each day and getting things done are challenges that nearly everyone faces. Most people don't want to do more—they want to do less. But doing less becomes an impossible goal when just getting through today's obligations can eat up every minute of the day—and then some.

The hundreds of ideas in this book can help you make some simple changes so you won't get caught up in an endless cycle of chores, duties and obligations. Part of each day, even if it's only a small part, should belong to you. Put even a few of the tips to work in your life and you'll streamline your day and get things done with less stress and in less time. You'll be able to do what you have to do so you have time to do what you want to do. After all, *now* is the time of your life. Why not use some of that time to live a little?

Getting Out the Door

"If everybody would do the things they needed to do to get out the door on time, instead of doing all the other things that they do do, we'd be ready on time. Sunday morning is the worst. In spite of my best efforts to help everyone, I'm always ready and in the car on time, and my wife and kids never are. I've had it. Starting next week, I'm leaving for church on time. If they're not ready, I'm leaving without them."

David Siefert, Father of five

Get Ready the Night Before

1

Spend ten minutes each night going over school papers your children bring home. Sign forms, check schedules, make notations and review homework assignments. You'll avoid a last-minute panic looking for important papers (such as permission slips) the following morning.

2

Keep all lunch-making materials in one place so it's easy to get lunches ready. Put tomorrow's lunches together tonight. Better yet, ask children who are old enough to pack their own lunch the night before.

3

Each day will get off to a better start if the kitchen is orderly. Tidy up after dinner. Run the dishwasher and empty it so it's ready for the breakfast dishes. Take out the trash. Set the breakfast table. Get the coffee ready so all you have to do is flip a switch. Divide kitchen chores among family members; everybody can do something.

4

Encourage children to do their part. Make a checklist of exactly what needs to be done at night and in the morning. Keep it simple and specific: Pack your knapsack, take out the trash, set the table for breakfast. Get dressed, brush your teeth, put the breakfast dishes in the dishwasher.

5

Have children select their breakfast the night before. Keep it simple by limiting the choices. They can decide between three cereals a lot quicker than six.

6

Insist that everyone pack up their own gear the night before. This includes homework and other paperwork, book bags, knapsacks, briefcases and purses. Get the diaper bag and baby gear together. Place the bags by the door so everyone can get going in an organized manner in the morning.

7

Straighten and pick up the house in the evening. It's easier to wake up in tidy surroundings, and you'll be able to get organized more easily in the morning if you aren't working your way past clutter at every step.

8

Decide today what you're going to wear tomorrow, including accessories. Make sure it's presentable before you go to bed.

9

Make sure each child has an appropriate outfit clean and ready to put on so you don't waste time in the morning fussing with them over what to wear and where to find that missing shoe.

10

Make it clear that some family members have to shower the night before. And those that shower in the morning have to be quick about it, or they get rotated to the nighttime shower schedule.

11

Get a good alarm clock and use it. Don't get a clock with a snooze button. Put the clock across the room; when it goes off, you have to get up to turn it off.

12

Go to bed. Don't stay up past your bedtime. You'll pay for it tomorrow when you won't want to get up on time.

Have a Launch Area by the Door

13

Establish a "parking zone" on a stand or hook near the door where you can keep your keys, briefcase and purse. Drop them there when you come in the door, and they'll be right there when you're ready to leave.

14

Keep things like book bags, boots, mittens and umbrellas by the door. If you have a large family, one bin or shelf and one hook for each person can help keep things ready to go in an orderly and responsible fashion.

15

If you'll be doing errands while you're out tomorrow, put what you need (such as the grocery list and the cleaning ticket) by the door.

Give Yourself Enough Time

16

Be realistic about the amount of time it takes to get out the door in the morning. Never try to do more than the time allows. It will only make you late.

17

Start early. The early bird really does get the worm.

18

Get up thirty minutes earlier and use that quiet time to read, write, exercise or pamper yourself. Your entire day will be better for this fresh start.

19

Make sure there are clocks in the bedroom, bathroom and kitchen so that everyone can be aware of the time at all times.

20

Add an extra fifteen minutes to your morning schedule in case something unexpected comes up. Add an extra fifteen minutes to your travel time for traffic or travel delays. And plan to get to your destination fifteen minutes early so you can organize your thoughts and ease into your day.

Have a Morning Routine

21

Make getting out the door a routine of specific tasks assigned to each member of the family. Post a schedule so everyone knows exactly what's expected of them and when.

22

Make sure you're up and dressed before you get the children up. When the children get up, have them get dressed before they come to breakfast. If chaos starts to creep in, at least everyone will be presentable and ready to go.

23

Group all breakfast foods together in the cupboard and refrigerator so that anyone can easily fix a bowl of cereal or toast and jelly.

24

Cut fussing time. Use a minimum amount of makeup (or none at all) and get a simple haircut that's easy to maintain.

25

To help cut down on the traffic jam in the bathroom, suggest that the females in the family apply makeup and dry their hair in another room. All that's needed is a mirror, a light and, if there's room, a small table. This makeup station can be set up in a corner in a large hall or bedroom.

26

If squabbles are breaking out among family members about time spent in the bathroom in the morning, draw up a bathroom schedule with a fixed amount of time allowed for each person. You can use a timer as an enforcement tool.

27

If you have a large family and only one bathroom, consider installing a second sink. Two people can get ready simultaneously, with half the bickering.

28

If you can't get family members going, set deadlines and enforce them with a kitchen timer. Fifteen minutes to shower and brush teeth. Ding! Fifteen minutes to get dressed. Ding! Twenty minutes to eat breakfast. Ding! Fifteen minutes to do morning chores. Ding! Ten minutes to get your things together and get your coat on. Ding!

29

Let everyone take responsibility for getting ready on time. Except for the very youngest, there's no reason why school-age children can't have an alarm clock and get themselves out of bed and ready to go. If they resist and hold everyone up, issue an ultimatum. Every morning that they don't get out the door on time equals one morning, afternoon or evening that they can't watch TV, talk on the phone or play with friends.

30

Don't answer the phone or turn on the TV in the morning. Before you know it you're late, simply because you were *distracted*. If you must answer the phone, at least turn on your answering machine twenty minutes before you plan to walk out the door, so you get going on time.

31

Walk out the door with plenty of time to get to your destination. Don't turn everyday hassles into crises. Being thrown off your schedule is not a crisis. Being in a car accident is.

Taking Control of
Your Day

"A hectic schedule is a lifestyle choice."
Elaine St. James, Author, Living the Simple Life

Budget Your Time

32

Schedule time for work, play, family and spiritual matters as well as regular time for yourself. A balanced lifestyle is more rewarding and usually lasts longer than an obsessive lifestyle.

33

Know what your priorities are, and plan your schedule with those priorities firmly fixed in your mind.

"Planning is key to achieving balance in my life. Every Sunday, I map out the next week for business, family and entertainment obligations and activities. Sometimes work gets more attention than family, and sometimes family gets more attention than work. But I find that with consistent attention to planning I can strike a balance so that over the course of a year no one area is unfairly shortchanged."
Rick J. Muth, President, Orco Block

34

Don't overcommit yourself. If you do, you won't have the re-
sources and energy to handle the everyday problems that can
balloon into crises.

Just Say No

*"I suffer from beyond the Zen of guilt; I apologize for things
that haven't even happened. So it's hard for me to say no.
But I've found that if I say yes to everyone, everything suffers.
So I practice the art of saying no every day. I say it gently,
but firmly, and I do it often."*

Fritz Coleman, Comedian and Television Weatherman

35

Resist the urge to be a super volunteer. Unless you have unlim-
ited time to spare, learn to say no to pleas from others that you
help out with "just one more thing." Determine how many
hours or days per month you can give to volunteer work, schedule that time and don't be afraid to let others know that you're
already "booked up."

36

Never agree to do something just to impress or please other
people. You can't please everyone, and worrying about the im-
pression you make is usually not a good use of your mental
energies.

37

Be selective about agreeing to social obligations. Don't get car-
ried away with the flattery of being asked when deep down you
know you'd rather be home with a good book. Say no. You
won't miss a thing.

38

Get all the details up front so you can gauge the full scope of what's being asked of you. What exactly will you be expected to do, and how often? Don't settle for vague descriptions. Feel free to decline all or part of the obligation.

39

Make your own plans your top priority. Say, "No, I'd love to help you, but I've already got five projects of my own to deal with." They'll not offer to help you with your projects. More likely, they'll beat a hasty retreat.

40

If you can't muster up the wherewithal to say no at the time of the request, stall. Say, "Let me think about that and get back to you." Wait a day or so, screw up your courage, and call back and say no.

41

Never say, "I don't have the time." People will inquire about your schedule in detail and then proceed to help you find the time they need. You'll end up saying yes in spite of yourself.

42

Don't discuss or defend your decision to say no. Develop some stock explanations that put the matter to rest, such as:
>"That's just not something I do."
>"I'm terrible at that; you'd better get someone else."
>"I make it a policy never to do that."
>"My husband/wife/accountant/lawyer would kill me if I agreed to that."
>"I've already got plans. Thanks anyway."
>"Sorry, maybe next time."

43

Don't go overboard and be a slave to the clock. Allow some room for personal spontaneity. Just because there's some white space on your calendar doesn't mean you need to fill it up.

44

Unexpected things come up—disasters as well as delights. Leave some room in your schedule to enjoy the good and deal with the bad.

45

Pad your schedule by at least an hour each day to absorb unexpected interruptions and unplanned activities that crop up.

Set a Schedule

46

Try to think ahead when you look at your schedule. If you're going to a special party next month, schedule time now to have your hair done. Don't wait to fit it in at the last minute.

47

If your schedule impacts others at work or home, make sure you go over your schedule with everyone at least once or twice a week.

48

Establish daily work routines. Make sales calls on Mondays, do your expense account on Tuesdays, do filing on Fridays, mow your yard on Saturdays and so on.

49

Schedule time to pay your bills regularly. Lapsed insurance and missed payments can be avoided with regularly scheduled time and attention to the necessary paperwork.

50

Schedule some time each week to spend getting organized, whether catching up on the laundry or doing your filing.

51

Schedule uninterrupted time for reading on a regular basis.

52

If you have a hard time sticking to an exercise schedule, try setting a regular date with a friend to work out together.

53

Schedule a catch-up day. Don't do anything except catch up. If you're way behind on all kinds of things, you might want to schedule a catch-up weekend, or several catch-up evenings.

54

If you have repairs that need to be done around the house, try to schedule them all on the same day instead of blocking out hours just to sit at home waiting for each repair person.

55

If you have a project you really want to do, but it will take a lot of time and you're too pooped at night to work on it, pretend you're working at a second job. You can work from seven to ten three nights a week or you can get up three hours earlier in the morning and pretend it's your first shift. Before you know it, you'll have that great American novel finished.

56

Once you've set your schedule, be careful about letting other people negotiate it with you. Selectively ignore suggestions that you add more to your schedule or change things around. Sometimes it's best to not even discuss it.

57

Don't be a slave to your time management system. Leave your schedule behind when you go out. When someone tries to pin you down with a request for your time, tell them you'll have to get back to them after you check your schedule. It gives you time to make a thoughtful decision and makes it easier for you to say no.

58

Make it a habit to review your calendar for the next few weeks at least every few days. Rearrange appointments and obligations if you see a roadblock forming.

Arrange Appointments Carefully

59

Get a good appointment book that you feel comfortable with. It's unrealistic to expect yourself to keep your entire schedule accurately in your head.

60

When you agree to an appointment, set a time limit up front. Say "I can give you a half hour from 9:00 to 9:30," for example. To make sure the appointment doesn't run over, keep an eye on the time, and at 9:25 announce that you'll have to "wrap things up."

61

When someone calls for an appointment with you, ask them to explain the reason for the meeting. Half the time you'll find that it can be handled over the phone, and you won't have to schedule an appointment after all.

62

If you want to make an appointment with someone, be specific about your request. "Could we get together for twenty minutes to go over some key points?" might be better received by a busy person than a request for "a meeting to discuss everything." Stick to your time limits. It'll help everyone keep to their schedules and make the best use of the time allotted.

63

Ask for the first appointment of the day. Unless your doctor or dentist is out saving a life, you should be able to get in without spending an eternity in the waiting room.

64

Just as medical professionals should be considerate of your time, so should you be considerate of theirs. Call in advance if you're going to be late or if you need to cancel your appointment. Jot down a list of symptoms or questions so you can get right to the point. Don't take along another patient for the doctor to look at "while she's at it."

65

Batch appointments. Schedule meetings with clients all on one day instead of seeing one on Tuesday, one on Wednesday and one on Friday. Schedule your children's medical checkups back-to-back in one day rather than extending the driving and inconvenience over several days.

66

If you see that you can't make an appointment, call to reschedule. Most people won't mind changing the date, as long as it isn't done at the last minute. If you're going to be late, call to see if your late arrival is acceptable. You may find that everybody would be happier to reschedule.

67

Don't agree to schedule something if you have no intention of getting there on time. If you don't really have the time to be on time, you probably shouldn't be scheduling it in the first place.

Allow for Waiting Time

68

When you make an appointment or reservation, ask if there's a wait, and don't hesitate to let the other party know that you don't like to wait. Say it nicely, but firmly. Often another time will be suggested when there'll be no wait.

69

Always carry something to read or do with you; when you're faced with unavoidable waits, you can catch up on some reading, write notes or letters, crochet or work a crossword puzzle.

70

If someone is more than twenty minutes late, leave. Unless the other party has called to explain their tardiness or to reschedule, it makes no sense for you to waste your time waiting. Leave word that you left after waiting twenty minutes. Eventually your reputation for punctuality will spread, and people will make a concerted effort to be on time for appointments with you.

71

If you spend an inordinate amount of time waiting for an appointment, consider sending a bill for your time. After all, time is money. Or, if people tend to cancel appointments with you at the last minute, you might want to charge them a cancellation fee. They'll be more considerate the next time.

72

If you have an appointment with any government agency, plan for bureaucratic delays. Allow lots of time, take plenty of reading material or a crossword puzzle with you, and muster up your reserve of patience.

73

When something opens (such as a popular movie or new play) wait a few weeks before you go. By then the demand will be less and the lines will be shorter.

74

Don't get in the habit of being late because you think you'll have to wait if you're early. You may have to wait even if you're late, and deliberately being late is rude.

75

Calm down. If waiting makes your blood pressure rise, learn to put a lid on it. Count to ten, pray, hypnotize yourself—whatever it takes to calm down. It's not worth giving yourself a heart attack.

Put Your Children on a Schedule

76

Don't sign your kids up for every activity that comes down the pike. You'll only run yourself ragged getting them to their scheduled destinations. If they need more to do, suggest they read a book or clean up the kitchen. You don't have to be the ultimate taxi driver and audience member, and they won't grow up to be criminals if they have only one or two extracurricular activities instead of four or five.

77

Have a Sunday meeting with the whole family to plan the week. Keep a large calendar posted where everyone can see it. Each member's schedule including special sports and school activities can be noted with a different colored pen.

78

If someone tries to add to your schedule at the last minute ("But I need brownies for the class party tomorrow!"), refuse to accommodate the request. Everyone will soon learn to plan ahead.

79

Enforce a strict homework schedule. If children know that they're expected to do their homework from five to seven each night before TV or telephone privileges, they'll learn to do it during the scheduled time without question.

80

Have a daily schedule for your kids. Let them know what time they're supposed to get into their pajamas, brush their teeth and be in bed. In the morning, reverse the schedule. Be specific, and post it if necessary. Keeping them on schedule makes it easier to manage your schedule better.

Review Your Day

81

At the end of each day, take a few minutes to review the day's accomplishments and remaining obligations so you can schedule tomorrow's most pressing priorities.

82

Figure out how many hours of sleep you need each night to feel rested, and then schedule your day to get that much sleep every night.

83

Take a few minutes every day to meditate or pray. While you're at it, count your blessings. It will put today and tomorrow into perspective.

"It's a challenge to be trustworthy stewards of the small moments of our lives."

Jimmy Carter, Former President of the United States

Working Smarter, Not Harder

"I start each day by identifying the three most important things to do, and I don't waste time worrying about the rest. If I get those three critical things done, I've had a productive day."

Charles H. James III, President and CEO, North American Produce

Plan and Organize Your Work Schedule

84

Schedule your work, especially where big projects are concerned. Set deadlines and stick to them.

85

Set aside uninterrupted time every day to do your paperwork so it won't back up on you.

86

Take some time to try to catch up on any backlogs. Come in early for a week or two, or spend a weekend getting it under control. You'll be able to handle daily obligations with less stress if you're not constantly worrying about things that have backed up on you.

87

If you work at home, set regular hours for yourself just as if you worked outside the house.

88

Don't take on more business than you can comfortably handle.

89

It's not necessary to work your fingers to the bone. It's also not necessary to be a clock watcher who lives for breaks and quitting time. Try to adopt a happy medium and your work day will be more balanced.

90

Organize your desk and keep it that way.

91

Have a separate basket for outgoing mail or finished projects that should be routed or filed. Clear the OUT basket several times a day.

92

Make sure you have an IN box so people can put in mail and other papers that arrive during the day. Check the box at least once or twice a day so you know what needs your attention.

93

Never keep work in progress inside desk drawers. It'll only get buried under your stationery and tea bags. Eventually, you'll forget about it altogether.

94

The next time you pick up a pen that doesn't write, throw it away. Don't put it back in the drawer like you always do.

95

Stop spreading your papers all over your desk; work on one piece of paper at a time and keep the rest neatly organized in a stack on a corner of the desk.

96

Keep a selection of office supplies within arm's reach. You won't have to rummage through the supply room or cabinet to find what you need.

97

Keep your briefcase or a tray marked HOME near your desk. Put any papers that need to go home with you in it. You'll reduce the clutter on your desk and, when you're ready to leave, you won't have to stop and think about what to take with you.

98

Clear your desk two or three times a day so the clutter doesn't get a foothold. The few minutes spent putting things in order will help clear your head. At the end of the day, stop ten minutes early to organize everything on your desk, and plan and prioritize your work for the following day.

99

Establish a routine to insure that the most important matters are taken care of as well as the daily must-do's such as opening the mail and returning phone calls.

100

Create systems and procedures for doing things. Make sure you review them periodically to update or streamline how things are done if changes occur.

101

If people travel to your office frequently, write clear directions along with your address, phone number and a small map. Keep copies on hand to mail or fax to people before they come.

102

Make it a routine to organize your expense report once a week, always on the same day. It won't snowball on you and you'll get your reimbursements closer to when you really need them.

103

Block out time to batch tasks. Allow a half hour first thing in the morning to check and answer e-mail. Return calls for one hour after lunch. Spend an uninterrupted hour each day on paperwork.

104

Don't hop up from your desk just to do one thing. Save up little "run-arounds" and do them all at once if you can.

105

Make sure you work on projects in order of priority. If you don't know which ones take priority, ask your supervisor.

106

Examine what you do in a day. Decide to stop wasting time working on something just because you're good at it and you like doing it. If it's not important, put it aside or delegate it so you can tackle what really matters.

107

Avoid duplication—from papers to efforts.

108

Don't waste time trying to reinvent the wheel. If something's already been done one way, and that way works, don't futz around trying to think of a new way to accomplish the same thing.

109

Make it a habit to follow up.

"I always ask for a person's business card and write the promised action on the back of the card as soon as I can. I follow through as soon as I get back to my office."
David C. Hochberg, Vice-President, Lillian Vernon Corporation

---

Show Some Initiative

110

Know how to do jobs other than your own. You'll be able to bail yourself out in an emergency (your secretary left unexpectedly) or put in for a promotion (you already know how to do parts of the job that'll be opening up).

111

Don't wait to be told what to do every step of the way. Be a self-starter. You'll have more control over your day, and you'll prove what a good employee you are at the same time.

112

If several people give you work to do throughout the day, clarify the chain of command. When you have more work than you can do in a day, you can prioritize whose work is more important.

113

Put together a team or task force if you need fresh ideas on how to be more productive or how to get a special project started.

Cut Down on Interruptions

114

When someone asks you if you have a minute, don't be afraid to say no.

115

Is there someone else who can help you? How long will this take? Ask yourself these questions when someone interrupts you to ask for help. If it's time-consuming, ask them to come back later. If someone else can help them, refer them to that person.

116

Ask constant interrupters to save all their interruptions for one small meeting each day.

117

People are less likely to step into your office if they can't make eye contact, so if you can, place your desk so you sit with your back to the door. Better yet, close the door.

118

Remove extra chairs from your office. People who like to drop by and chat will be less likely to do so since there's no way to do it comfortably.

119

Try to avoid storing information in your office that others need to see regularly. Your office will start to take on the tone of a library, with people popping in and out saying, "I just need to see that XYZ manual."

"I get up at five A.M. Most people don't realize what an incredible time of day that is. If I had more time, I'd go out for a bit; the streets provide the perfect silent backdrop to the sunrise. I get to work before anyone else does—at about 6:30 A.M. With no interruptions, I can organize my desk, plan my day, and get a head start on my work. One of the first things I always do is deal with any overdrafts. I like to call those people bright and early so they have plenty of time to get to the bank with their money before the day is over."

Carol Jones, Vice-President and Manager, First Pacific National Bank

---

120

Set aside blocks of "do not disturb" time. Close the door and insist that, unless it's an emergency, you're not to be disturbed. If you don't have an office with a door you can close, leave your desk. Find an office or conference room that's temporarily vacant and hole up for an hour or two.

Keep Drop-Ins to a Minimum

121

If someone drops in to your office unexpectedly, immediately stand up. It's a hint that's hard to miss. If necessary, start walking out. Tell the person you were just leaving and ask if you can talk as you walk.

"If someone in the company wants to discuss a serious legal or financial issue, I'll stop and talk with them. Most of the time, the question can be turned over to someone else in the company. If that's not appropriate, I'll tell the person to solve it on their own by using their best judgment. People don't always do things exactly the way I would have, but most of the time, it's not that big of a deal. Gradually, people have learned to try to solve their problems either through other avenues or on their own; dropping by my office should always be reserved for only the most important issues or as a last resort."

Simon Grill, President, Mr. Vend Manufacturing Co.

122

Set parameters at the beginning. When a drop-in visitor says he needs to talk with you, say, "Fine, but I've only got about five minutes to give you right now."

123

When someone stops by to discuss something, tell her you're busy right now, but can stop by her desk in about twenty minutes. It's much easier to exit someone else's work area without wasting time than it is to get them out of yours.

124

Don't let the drop-in visitor get off the subject. Stick to the topic at hand, and don't be tempted into digressing to other subjects, such as how incompetent George is or the results of last night's ball game.

125

If you start to answer a question and your answer leads to another question, then another, cut the conversation short. Say, "You know, this is a bit more complicated than I thought, and it needs more than a few minutes to be discussed properly. I'm in the middle of something right now. Let's make another time to get together and discuss it."

126

When a visitor drops in, announce to your assistant or to a colleague when you'll be done. Say, "We'll only be about fifteen minutes," and make sure your visitor hears you say it.

127

If you know you're going to be interrupted by a chronic windbag, prearrange with a co-worker to come into your office and "remind" you of another appointment in five minutes.

128

If someone is stopping by your desk for socializing purposes only, and you want to socialize, but need to get your work done, arrange to meet them on your coffee break or at lunchtime.

129

When someone interrupts you in the middle of a tedious chore, don't stop. Get them to help you instead. If you're in the middle of a big mailing, ask them to seal envelopes while you stamp them. (You can talk as you do this.) Asking for help can make even the most chronic interrupter think twice before taking up your time.

130

If you want to get rid of a visitor who's dropped in and stayed too long, try looking at your watch every few minutes and see if they take the hint.

131

If someone from outside the office stops by unannounced and he's not an important client, don't invite him into your office. Meet in the reception area or the hall. Most people will either get right to the point, or mumble something about just being in the neighborhood, and then depart.

Don't Interrupt Yourself

132

Don't tackle the mail the minute it arrives if you're in the middle of something else. Opening the mail when you should be finishing a sales report is just an excuse to interrupt yourself and procrastinate.

133

Don't allow daily or mundane interruptions to assume the urgent mantle. A constantly ringing telephone can be ignored. Let voice mail take some messages while you take care of more important priorities.

134

Recognize when you're welcoming the interruption of a phone call. Then don't blame your dashed schedule on the phone calls. Blame it on yourself.

135

Don't come to a complete stop just because something else has. You don't have to "help" the computer or washer repair person. You can open your mail, sort papers, make phone calls or tidy up while he gets it going again for you.

Keep Meetings Short and to the Point

136

Don't schedule a meeting unless you have the objective *clearly defined* and *written down*. Keep the meeting on track so its objective can be achieved.

137

Have meetings either first thing in the morning when everyone is eager to get on with their day, or at the end of the day when everyone is anxious to leave.

138

Distribute a detailed agenda in advance of the meeting. Along with the points to be discussed, you'll want to list the decisions to be made and the problems to be solved. Allocate a specific amount of time for each topic and let everyone know what that amount is.

139

Keep it short. Short meetings are generally more effective than long affairs. Never let a meeting run over two hours.

140

If you want a meeting to go really quickly, remove the chairs in the room.

141

Let everyone know, in advance, what time the meeting will be over. Then make sure you end it on time.

142

Keep the number of participants in the meeting to a minimum. The more people in attendance, the more time-consuming the meeting will become.

143

Start the meeting on time. Don't wait for anyone. Don't review material that's already been covered for latecomers. (If you want to make sure that people arrive at meetings on time, make the last person who arrives take minutes.)

144

Be specific about time. When you announce a coffee break, don't be vague about its length. Instead of saying, "Let's take a break of about fifteen minutes or so," say, "Let's break now and reconvene promptly at 10:30."

145

Don't allocate meeting time to read documents and reports. Written materials that pertain to the subject at hand should be circulated in advance for participants to read before the meeting.

146

Don't let meetings turn into a bull session or a coffee klatch. Stick to the agenda; socializing can be done *after* the meeting.

147

Stay on schedule. If people tend to spend the first ten or fifteen minutes of a meeting chatting, get people going by checking your watch and announcing the time to the room: "It's 9:30. Let's get started."

148

Before you automatically make plans to attend a meeting, ask if it's really necessary for you to be there. If it isn't, try to get out of it.

149

If there are several topics of discussion at a meeting and only one concerns you, see if you can leave once that issue has been addressed.

150

Don't ramble during the meeting. It wastes time and drives everyone crazy. If others can't get to the point, help them along by suggesting a vote on the issue or by tabling the topic for the next meeting's agenda.

151

If you must meet with someone over a meal, do it at breakfast rather than lunch or after work. Breakfast meetings tend to take up less time because everyone has to get on with their day. Lunch and after-work meetings tend to drag on in direct proportion to the amount of alcohol consumed and the lack of motivation to get back to work or home.

152

If your lunch meetings tend to be too sociable or meander more than you'd like, consider meeting first at your office for thirty minutes to go over the more important business, and then go to lunch. This way, if social chitchat takes over at lunch, you've gotten the more important business of the meeting behind you.

153

If you must meet in a restaurant, ask for the check when the waiter brings the food so you won't have to chase it.

Use Your Computer Efficiently

154

Stop saying you'll do something "as soon as you get a computer." Do it now. The old way has worked all this time; it will continue to work until you really do get a computer.

155

Don't be blind to the fact that some tasks can be done faster by hand than by computer.

156

If you want to learn the basics on your computer, start by asking your kids. They can probably teach you a thing or two.

157

Don't expect computers to make your life paperless. Computers can generate far more paper than you ever had in the first place, because it's so much easier to generate. Learn to keep your finger off the print button.

158

Computers won't save you time if you're constantly upgrading equipment and software. You'll spend most of your time in the learning mode which, in real terms, produces nothing.

159

If you really want to turn your computer into a productive tool, remove all the games.

160

Don't waste time entering trivia into the computer.

161

Don't use the computer to compulsively edit and rewrite documents.

162

Keep any information you generate short and to the point. Don't let your computer seduce you into producing more material and more copies than anyone needs or wants.

163

Don't spend more time than necessary formatting or fiddling with fonts, graphics or colors.

164

Don't try to be the ultimate master of your computer. If you can't get something to work, don't waste time futzing and tinkering. Ask for help immediately.

165

Don't get sucked into "chat" rooms on the Internet. If you want to chat, talk to your neighbors, your friends and your family.

166

Resist the temptation to become addicted to the computer. You have better things to do.

Organize Your Work Area

167

Stop putting papers in piles "just for now" because you can't make a decision about what to do with them. You'll only keep reading and rereading the papers on your desk as you shuffle them from one pile to another. Read it, decide on a course of action, then move it or do it.

168

Remember that the top of your desk is a work area, not an archive. Don't keep papers on your desk that are headed for the filing cabinet or the trash.

169

If you put a two-drawer filing cabinet next to your desk you'll be able to keep important files and materials at your fingertips.

170

If you frequently work on projects that result in lots of bulky papers, establish a project area for those papers. It can be a table, credenza, or rolling file cart. When the project is completed, transfer the papers and files to file boxes for storage.

171

Keep forms that you use regularly within arm's reach. Some hanging folders in your desk or credenza drawer should do the trick.

172

Never keep office supplies in the filing cabinet. Supplies belong in the supply cabinet or closet, not in the records and information storage area.

173

Don't use a bulletin board. It will only become a hanging burial ground for paper clutter.

174

Keep a large trash can near your desk or work area. Make good use of it every day.

Eliminate Unnecessary Paperwork

Ask yourself if you are in the paperwork business. Is your job a clerical one? Is you income generated primarily from administrative work? If the answer is no to any of the above, you might want to follow my Rule Number One? Never do paperwork unless this is your primary business. Make it go away by delegating it."

Betty Jo Tilley, Realtor

175

If you've got more than one To Do list, you have too many. Don't keep old, expired lists. Keep only one list for the here and now.

176

Don't ask for information you don't need. Overcome information anxiety. Limit the amount of information you receive and try to absorb. Stop feeling guilty about information that's beyond your limits.

177

If you have to respond to someone in writing, keep your response brief and to the point.

178

Keep sample letters that you can use as a format for routine correspondence. Use form letters whenever possible.

179

If you are routinely copied on reports, memos or letters that you really don't need, see if you can get your name off the routing list.

180

If you must read voluminous business documents and journals, use a highlighter the first time you read one. Highlight key items, and the next time you pick up the document you won't have to reread it to locate the vital information.

181

Keep report writing and reading to the minimum. People who want to bamboozle others often do it with pages and pages of poppycock that looks good but means nothing. Don't do it yourself, and ask others to stop as well.

182

Try to whittle away the number of reports you have to deal with: Don't bother reading any for a few weeks and see if anybody cares. Don't send any and see if anybody notices.

183

Include one-page outlines or recaps of lengthy documents you send out so everyone can grasp the key points immediately. Ask others to do the same.

184

If you create drafts of documents before you put out a final copy, type each draft on a different color paper so you can tell them apart. Don't keep every draft forever, and don't keep creating drafts until the cows come home.

185

Resist the urge to add to your disorder by compulsively making notes on dozens of different pieces of paper and notepads. Keep them in one notebook or binder.

186

Resist the urge to make multiple copies of everything. Every time you copy something on a duplicating machine, you're contributing to the blizzard of papers blanketing the human race.

187

Don't have a "pending" file. *Pending* is just another word for "I don't know what to do with this, so I'll just put it here for now." *Pending* also means "It'll get done de-pending on when I get around to it," which is usually never.

188

Ask yourself how you can get rid of every piece of paper that comes your way. Toss it, act on it, file it, or pass it on—as soon as you possibly can.

Open and Sort Your Mail

"I receive a ton of mail on a daily basis. Of course I can't possibly deal with it all immediately. So I prioritize it three ways: must do within 48 hours; must do this week; and must do this year. To those who have to wait a year to hear from me, I offer my strongest apologies and beg for forgiveness. I must say that I don't usually hear back from those people. . . . I think that's terribly rude, don't you?"

Letitia Baldrige, Authority on behavior

189

Establish a "mail center," whether it's a bin, a table or a specific spot on a counter. Make sure you put your mail there every day as it comes in.

190

If you tend to get caught up in the day's events and overlook the mail, set a time every day when you will open and sort it. You can do it right after lunch, for example, or right after your morning break.

"Remind yourself that when you die, your IN Basket won't be empty."

Richard Carlson, Author, Don't Sweat the Small Stuff

191

When you open your mail, toss the junk inserts that come with bills. Sort the opened mail into four bins: *To Do*, *To Pay*, *To File* and *To Read*. You can get back to the mail later. In the meantime, at least it's been opened and sorted.

192

Use a letter opener. It helps move things along. Really.

Don't Let E-Mail Overwhelm You

"I handle e-mail by setting up filters on my computer, based on key people I need to respond to right away. All other e-mail is filtered out for my assistant to review. I get through e-mail faster if I ignore the phone while I'm reading and responding to the day's communications. And after the second reply on e-mail, I make it a point to either pick up the phone or walk over to that person's office so that I don't lose the personal touch."

Alan Gleicher, Senior Vice-President, INTUIT

193

Just because mail arrives on a computer doesn't mean you have to drop everything and "open" it immediately. E-mail can wait, just like the mail in your IN box can wait. You'll get to it when you get to it.

194

Resist the urge to go hog-wild sending every little thing that pops into your head to everybody via e-mail. Eliminate your e-mail habit and ask others to do the same.

195

Don't get overwhelmed by e-mail. It's no different than regular mail; half of it is junk.

Get Rid of Junk Mail

196

If you pick up your mail at the post office, take a few minutes and quickly sort through the stack while you're there. Leave all junk mail behind—in the post office trash or recycling can.

197

Don't even think about thumbing through junk mail. Toss it immediately.

198

Open your mail near a trash can. Make sure it's a *roomy* one. Dinky, fancy trash cans have no business in an office or desk area. One day's junk mail will topple such a boudoir basket.

199

If you insist on reading junk mail, set it aside to read during low-energy times. Use prime time for dealing with important mail.

200

Get your name off mailing lists so you don't get junk mail in the first place.

Move the Mail Along

201

If you have a secretary, let that person open, sort and screen your incoming mail. There's a lot of paperwork that you probably never have to see in the first place.

202

Date papers when they come in the mail so you can prioritize effectively.

203

Route things immediately. If you get a journal to read and you're one of six people on the routing list, read it and move it along. If you don't have time to read it, move it along, and add your name again at the bottom of the routing slip.

204

Unless you really need to read the journal that's routed to five other people, take your name off the routing list.

205

Routing slips should have a final destination listed on the last line. If it's the trash instead of the file, say so. The last person who gets the material tosses it when they're finished.

206

Keep your love letters forever. But keep them to yourself.

Set Up Simple Systems at Home

207

If you handle paperwork at home, establish a work area solely for the purpose of doing and storing paperwork.

208

Set up a central location at home where everybody can deposit the mail, phone messages and reminder notes for family members.

209

Make your own "House Directory" in a three-ring binder. Include important phone numbers for repair services, baby-sitters, restaurants, emergencies and other numbers that you call regularly.

210

Make a copy of your address book, particularly if that's the only place that you keep important phone numbers.

211

Make a master list of all your credit card numbers. Note the limit for each card as well as the customer service number. This reference sheet will come in handy when you want to check your limit or report a loss or theft.

212

Stick to using only one or two credit cards. You'll have less to carry around in your wallet, and your mail and paperwork will be reduced accordingly.

213

Photocopy the contents of your wallet. If you lose it, it'll be easier to replace important credit cards and other documents.

Make Things Easy to File and Find

214

Keep a large box or basket for items that need to be filed. Put it behind or under your desk so you don't have to shuffle past inactive paperwork and files all day.

215

Unfold papers before you file them; never put them into the file inside an envelope.

216

Put the most recent piece of paper in front of the other papers in the file so the file stays in chronological order.

217

Staple papers that are to be filed rather than use paper clips. Paper clips catch onto other papers and take up too much space.

218

Use a hanging file system for your files.

219

The plastic hanging folder tab goes on the front of the folder, not the back. Stagger each tab so you can see all the files at a glance when you open the drawer.

220

Always put a manila folder inside the hanging folder in your filing cabinet.

221

Never remove the hanging file folder from the drawer.

222

Create as few categories as possible in your filing system and use a simple alphabetical system for filing within those categories. Make your file identification labels consistent and easy to understand.

223

Don't index your files—it's usually an unnecessary step. If you must have a cross-referencing system, a simple "see also" notation written directly on the inside of the file folder jacket should suffice.

224

Resist the urge to color-code your files. It adds complications and requires special supplies.

225

Make sure your filing system is so simple that anyone can understand and work with it.

226

Don't set up files marked "miscellaneous." They become dumping grounds for papers that should be tossed or filed elsewhere.

227

Keep some file folders at your fingertips so you can make up a file as soon as you have paperwork accumulating that's not related to existing files.

228

When file folders get full, use the lines at the bottom of file folders (both manila and hanging) to expand the folder. Simply crease at the line, and the folder will hold more papers.

229

If a file becomes bulky, break it down by category, name or date. One huge file can be turned into several files, each smaller and easier to deal with than the original.

230

Don't overstuff your filing cabinet drawers. You should have at least four inches of extra space in each drawer to allow easy access and full visibility to all the files in the drawer.

231

If your filing cabinet gets full, don't buy another one; clean out the one you have and organize what's in it, and you'll probably have all the room you need.

232

Use three-ring binders to store and transport papers. Binders can hold committee reports and minutes, financial records, address lists, and warranties and instructions.

233

Cut down on copying and circulating reference materials by using binders to store information that's commonly used. Put the binders in an area where everyone can reference the material.

234

Don't file junk or bulky items. Store bulky items, such as trade journals, in bookcases rather than in files.

235

Circle, highlight or attach a note to papers to indicate the name and category the papers should be filed under. Anyone can do your filing for you without reading your mind. Once filed, you should be able to find papers again on your own.

236

Eliminate duplications and consolidate files. Periodically review the files in your cabinet. Catch mistakes. You might have a file marked "Insurance—Health" under "I" and one marked "Health Insurance" under "H." Neither file would provide a complete picture for you.

237

If you can't find a piece of paper or a file, it could be misfiled. Look in the folder in front of, and in back of, where the file is supposed to be in the drawer. Check everybody's desktop and To File bin, since nearly everyone procrastinates when it comes to filing. Chances are, you'll find what you're looking for.

238

Box inactive papers and files. Label the front of the box with the exact contents and the date. If possible, add a date when the contents can be destroyed. Store the boxes and review and purge yearly.

239

File regularly—daily if you can. A filing system is useless if you ignore it and pile instead of file.

240

On the other hand, stop automatically filing so much paper. Remember that 80 percent of everything you file you never look at again.

Make Choices and Changes

241

Think back. When you were nineteen, you were probably twice as happy, with half as much stuff. You had almost no paperwork. Every day brings a new opportunity to make choices and changes. Just for today, choose to simplify your life by eliminating at least some of the paperwork that complicates your life.

242

Stop working fifteen minutes before you go home each day. Use that time to organize your desk and choose tomorrow's priorities.

243

Treat others the way you'd like to be treated. Be productive and responsible for your work. Approach your work, your clients and your colleagues in a friendly but professional manner. Your day will be better for it.

Getting Things Done

"Lord, help me to sort out what I should do first, second and third today and to not try to do everything at once and nothing well. Give me the wisdom to delegate what I can, to say no when I need to, and the sense to know when to go home."

Marion Wright Edelman

Prioritize and Plan

244

Everyone has the same twenty-four hours in a day. People who prioritize and plan get more done than those who don't. Not everyone and everything is equally important. Prioritize on a daily as well as a long-term basis. Write your priorities down.

245

Review your priorities every day. Begin the day by tackling a high priority item. Leave low priority items for last. At the end of the day if you didn't get everything done, it should be the less important tasks that are left to do.

246

Bear in mind that what you do today may have a direct impact on how much you may have to do tomorrow.

247

Don't automatically assign a high priority to tasks that others have asked you to do. Let their request take its proper place on your list of things to do. It's up to you to assign the priority level.

248

Don't stoop to doing busywork just to seem active or productive. Keep your priorities in mind, and you'll get the things done that really should be done.

249

Stop fantasizing that you'll get everything done. There's always something to do. Eliminate excess obligations where you can, delegate as much as possible, and define and enthusiastically work on your priorities in life. Let some of the rest of it go.

250

Make it a point to continually reevaluate your priorities. Life is not a dress rehearsal.

251

Make sure you plan tomorrow today, before all your tomorrows get away from you. Lurching from day to day never produces much over the long haul. Good things rarely just "happen." Remember the adage: Fail to plan, plan to fail.

252

Don't underestimate the amount of time it will take to complete a project or task. Be realistic, not fantastic.

253

If someone tells you a project will take one hour, silently add thirty minutes for idiot time since, somewhere along the line, some idiot will probably mess things up so that the project actually takes longer to do.

254

Set deadlines for yourself. Let others know you're "on deadline" and work in that mode until you're done.

255

Don't be at the mercy of others to get things done. Set deadlines for them. Say "If I don't hear from you by next Friday, I'll assume that I can send the report on as is."

256

If others lag behind in getting things done, set an artificial deadline that's earlier than the real deadline. When you really need to have something, it should be ready.

257

Inch by inch, it's a cinch. Break large projects into smaller, manageable segments. Work on one segment at a time. Before you know it, you'll be done.

258

Allow enough time to do it right the first time. You'll save the time you would have spent if you'd done it poorly and had to do it over.

259

Always ask yourself what could go wrong. Embrace Plan A with enthusiasm, but always have a solid Plan B ready to go.

260

Stick to your plans. Don't let others cajole you into doing something you don't want to do.

261

Don't forget to plan for pleasure. Then revel in it.

Write Things Down

262

If you need to remember something—whether it's an appointment, an errand or a great idea—write it down. It provides a visual reminder system for you and clears your mind for creative ideas.

263

Organize your To Do list. Review and reprioritize it daily. Cross off completed tasks. Add any new items. Don't waste time rewriting your list every day; rewrite it once or twice a week.

264

If you're working on a big project, when you stop for the day, write down exactly what you need to do next. It makes it easier to get started when you pick the project back up again.

265

Keep notes and take them with you. Write an exact description of the noise your car is making when it happens so you can remember it when you take the car in; keep notes of questions and comments you need to address at the next sales meeting. You won't forget anything, and you'll accomplish more.

Be Decisive

266

Don't waste time stalling, waffling or making excuses, when all that's needed is a simple decision to get started.

267

Keep choices to a minimum. The more choices you have, the longer it takes to make a decision. The longer it takes to make a decision, the longer it takes to get things done.

268

If you can't decide because you really aren't the best person to make the decision, let someone else decide for you so you can get on with things.

Get a Good Start

269

Don't put off until tomorrow what you can do today, especially since you know you probably won't do it tomorrow anyway.

270

Stop using money as an excuse. If you wait until you can afford to do something, you'll never do it. Figure out how to take the first step in spite of money, and then get going.

271

Quit procrastinating. Stop fussing about where to start. Just start.

272

Start by doing the worst first, and the rest of the day will be downhill for you.

273

Start on time, even if others are late. Don't bother to rehash conversations that have taken place before their arrival, and don't reheat dinner for latecomers.

Follow Daily Do's and Don'ts

274

Always ask yourself if there's a simpler way to get something done. If there is, do it that way.

275

Help, don't hinder, and ask others to do the same.

276

Be specific.

"I'm specific, and I like others to be specific as well. It helps eliminate time-consuming confusion and unnecessary miscommunication. When everyone is specific, things tend to get done with 'first-time' accuracy and dispatch."
Frank Biondi, Chairman and CEO, Universal Studios, Inc.

277

Don't bite off more than you can chew. Stop agreeing to take on every project that comes along. Take on only what you can comfortably accomplish or what you're absolutely obligated to do.

278

Don't agree to do anything that's more trouble than it's worth.

279

Fix things that always slow you down. When a drawer sticks, fix it. If your child stopped riding his/her bike to school because it broke down, fix it so you don't have to be the daily chauffeur.

280

Do your important work during your prime energy time. Save mundane matters for the time of day when you've the least amount of energy.

281

Don't start any new projects if you've a lot of half-done projects already in progress. Finish one of those first.

282

Don't leave half-finished projects strewn about. When you stop, mark where you stopped and what comes next, and put things away. When you return to the project you'll be glad for the fresh start.

283

Don't scatter your time and efforts by always stepping in to do someone else's job or chores because they're procrastinating or doing a poor job. That's their responsibility, not yours. You've got enough to do.

284

Quit while you're ahead. Try to pick a good place to stop, rather than stopping in the middle of something. It'll be much easier to start up again later.

285

Don't start what you can't finish. Always finish what you start.

Quit Nitpicking and Just Do It

286

Stop putting things off until you can find the perfect time, the perfect place or the perfect way to get it done. Learn to compromise. The world won't come to an end, and you'll get a lot more done.

287

Stop insisting that every task be done perfectly. The house doesn't have to be perfectly kept, and you don't need to rewrite a business letter five times to get it just right. Perfect is not the same as excellent, and sometimes good is good enough.

288

Learn to recognize when enough is enough. Use the "going down for the third time" rule—if you've done something over three times, it's probably time to let it go.

289

If you can't get past the feeling you have to do every little thing perfectly, slowly force yourself to stop. Every day let at least one thing get done well, but not perfectly.

290

Stop waiting for a huge chunk of time to become available before you get started on something that needs to be done. Major blocks of time are few and far between. Chip away at things you have to do. Remember that doing something is always better than doing nothing at all.

291

The next time you find yourself caught up in wishing ("I wish I could . . . I wish I had . . . I wish I knew . . ."), try to put those wishes into action. Stop wishing so much, and start doing more.

292

Don't get stuck in the discussion stage. Move on to the action stage.

293

Don't ignore small tasks that only take a few minutes to do. File regularly. Pay bills weekly. Put things away, right away. Establish daily habits and routines to "do it now" so small things don't turn into a mountain of tedious chores.

294

Stop waiting until the last minute to do things because you think you work best under pressure. Extra stress never helped anybody or anything, and waiting for pressure to kick in is a poor excuse for not getting down to work when you should.

Don't Get Sidetracked

295

Cut to the chase. Don't let people, including yourself, waste time by beating around the bush. Get to the point to get things done.

296

Do first things first. Don't let others sidetrack you with their demands. You don't have to do everything for everybody the minute they ask you to.

297

Don't allow distractions—from telephone calls to dishes in the sink to drop-in visitors. Stick with the job at hand. You can always get back to the callers, the dishes and the visitors when you're done.

298

Concentrate on the matter at hand. Complete one task before you tackle another.

299

Don't get caught up in minutiae. Tackle the major components of any project first; fine-tune the details later.

300

Resist the temptation to lose yourself in research. Seeking more information than you really need is a form of procrastination that delays the action you need to take or the results you're required to achieve.

301

Don't waste time obsessing about problems. Solve problems, don't make them.

Know When to Give Up

302

Have a clear picture in your mind of the benefits of getting things done. If there are no benefits, maybe you don't have to do it, or maybe someone else can do it.

303

Be realistic about how much you can do. If you always find yourself surrounded by half-finished projects, it's time for you to let go of the idea that you can do so much.

304

Negotiate what and how much you can do. You can't be everything to everybody, and you can't do everything all the time.

305

Do you really have to do this? If you find yourself constantly procrastinating, delegate it. Maybe the task no longer relates to your priorities. Perhaps it doesn't have to be done at all. Give yourself permission to let it go.

306

Ask yourself what's the worst that'll happen if you don't do something. If the consequences aren't dire, eliminate it from your list of priorities or postpone it indefinitely. Put your energies into more important pursuits, and stop worrying about undone trivial tasks.

307

If you find yourself not doing a particularly distasteful task, find someone else to do it for you so it gets done once and for all.

308

Don't let the fear of making a mistake keep you at something long after it should have been deep-sixed. Sometimes a mistake is just another way of doing things. Learn from it. Cut your losses and move on.

309

Know when to quit. When you see that something is pointless, bail out and move on.

Delegate

310

Stop thinking that if you want something done right, you'll have to do it yourself. Almost every task can be delegated and, with a little training, can be completed successfully by someone other than yourself.

311

Stop being a know-it-all. Sometimes the only way to get things done is to hire an expert.

312

Stop thinking it's a sign of weakness to delegate. It's a sign of responsibility, vision and good common sense.

313

Stop saying that it's easier to do it yourself. If it's so easy, why haven't you done it already?

314

Don't be put off by the amount of time it'll take to train someone. That training time could pay off in a big way later when you'll get twice as much done in half the time.

315

Remember that controlling and doing everything yourself does not necessarily make you important. Mostly it just makes you anxious and tired all the time.

316

Stop refusing to delegate so that you'll be seen as a hero for doing everything. Real heroes save lives. You might get a pat on the back, but don't delude yourself. You're no hero.

"It takes no genius to observe that a one-man band never gets very big. To conduct a symphony you have to let others play. . . . A peak performer delegates to other people in order to multiply his or her own strengths."

Charles Garfield, Author, Peak Performances

317

Don't delegate just so you can feel important. True importance comes from more than arbitrarily telling others what to do. Delegate, don't dictate.

318

Don't delegate what you can eliminate. It's not productive.

319

Don't fib about the nature of the task being delegated. If it's drudgery, don't pretend that it's glamorous. Don't confuse delegating with dumping. People know when they're being dumped on, and they'll resent it.

320

Don't delegate responsibility without also granting some authority. Without at least minimal authority, a person can only work in frustrating fits and starts. Productivity and quality can suffer as a result.

321

Focus on what needs to be done rather than how it should be done. Stop micromanaging everything. You'll only drive yourself, and everyone around you, crazy and get half as much done as you should.

322

Break tasks down into manageable steps and write them down. Having expectations clearly defined on paper helps reduce miscommunication and gets things done.

323

Don't delegate late in the day unless it's absolutely necessary. Receiving extra things to do late in the day irritates people.

324

Keep a list of tasks and projects you've delegated to others so you know what you don't have to do.

325

Be available for occasional questions. Establish periodic review times to check progress and catch any shortfall while it can still be corrected.

326

Nip time-consuming problems in the bud. Make sure people know they can bring you bad news as soon as it develops. Hearing bad news early on makes it easy to correct the course of action before things compound into a situation where nothing can be done.

327

Reinforce positive results in others with thanks and frequent praise.

328

Never lose sight of the fact that no one person can do everything. This means you.

Use Telephone Timesavers

329

Keep track of calls you need to make by writing each one, along with the phone number, on an index card. When you're ready to call, organize the To Call cards by priority, starting with the most important calls.

330

Make sure you know what you're going to say and what points you need to cover *before* you make a call. Make a few notes for yourself and have all the necessary information close at hand. You'll be able to finish all of your business in one call instead of two or three.

331

If you make sales calls, or receive calls from potential clients, develop a brief script so you won't forget to ask the necessary questions or pass along the proper information.

332

If you make long-distance calls to friends or relatives and tend to forget things you meant to tell them, keep a brief list of things you want to talk about as you think of them. When you call (or when they call you) you won't forget anything.

333

Rather than stopping several times during the day to make one or two calls, make half a dozen calls and callbacks during the morning and another batch later in the day. It helps avoid the backlog and bruised feelings that develop when calls aren't made or returned.

334

Group your calls according to purpose: Make all your scheduling calls at one time, and place all your orders at another time. You'll get through a stack of calls quickly and feel like you've accomplished something.

335

Cluster your calls according to your mood. If you have to make a lot of sales calls that require you to be chatty and upbeat, do them when you have the most energy. Save low energy times for calls that are mundane, like making appointments or requesting routine information.

336

If you need important information, make those calls early in the day so the people you contact have time to assemble the information and get back to you before day's end.

337

Make phone calls right before lunch or at the end of the day when the person you're calling will be anxious to get off the phone.

338

If you want to take care of an important matter by phone, and you know the call will be lengthy, set up a telephone appointment with the other party. Block it on your calendar just as you would any appointment.

339

When information needs to be exchanged in a call, take care of that business first so if either of you has to suddenly end the call, at least the most important issue's been addressed.

340

Don't waste time on hold. If someone asks if they can put you on hold, say no. Give them your number and ask them to call you back within fifteen minutes.

341

When someone asks if this is a good time to call—and it isn't—say so. Offer to call back later or ask the person to call you at another time.

Make Messages Count

342

To remember something when you are out of the office, simply call your own answering machine or voice mail and leave a message. When you get back, you'll play your messages and hear your own reminder.

343

When you ask someone to call you, make sure you include the best time to reach you. Give broad guidelines rather than overly specific times. Saying "early morning or late in the day" is much more reasonable than instructing someone to call you between 8:15 and 9:00 A.M.

344

If you're faced with leaving a message, ask if someone else can help you instead.

345

When you call someone, announce yourself completely and state the purpose of your call. If you're returning a call, say so. Providing complete information can help you get through to your party quicker. If you have to leave a message, the person who returns your call will be more likely to be ready with the information you need.

346

Whenever you leave a message for someone, make it a point to ask the name of the person taking the message. This request makes just enough of an impact on the message-taker to help guarantee your message will get through.

347

When you take someone's phone number, make sure you get their extension number. If you have to leave a message on their voice mail, you'll be able to immediately enter their extension number and save yourself time listening to a long menu of options.

348

If you have to leave a message on someone's voice mail, repeat your phone number twice so they won't have to stop and back up the tape if they missed it the first time. Make sure you leave your full name since the person you're calling may know more than one Tom, Dick or Harry.

349

Don't waste too much time attempting to return someone else's call. If you return the call twice and can't reach them, leave a message and forget about it. If they really need to reach you, they will.

350

If you've tried several times without success to reach someone by phone, then fax or mail your message to the person. Don't call to see if the fax or message arrived. Often they'll respond with the information you need, and you'll save yourself the time and frustration involved in constantly calling back.

351

When you're returning calls and end up leaving a message rather than reaching the person, make a note on the call slip to indicate that you left a message. You'll be able to keep track of calls that have been made or returned, even if you didn't reach anyone.

Put Calls on Hold

352

Establish hard-and-fast rules about not answering the phone or making phone calls during certain times. Never answer the phone on Sunday mornings, for example. You'll find yourself looking forward to those little bits of phone peace.

353

If you have a project to complete, don't return any calls (unless it's a true emergency). Change your answering machine message to let people know you'll be unavailable. You'll find that half the time they don't even leave a message since, the truth is, the call was unnecessary in the first place.

354

Honor the time it takes to slip into an intense concentration mode for special projects and don't let the phone interrupt you when you're in that mind-set. If you do, you'll have to start all over to get back to where you were.

355

Let voice mail handle your calls for blocks of concentration time that you need. You'll get more done in less time because you won't be stopping and starting so much.

356

If you need uninterrupted time to get important work done, try to arrange an exchange of phone-answering duties. Someone else will answer your phones in the morning, and you'll answer theirs in the afternoon.

357

If you work at home, get one line for your business calls and a separate unlisted line for personal calls you might get in the evenings and on weekends. Protect your private number at all costs. Never give it out to anyone but your closest friends and family.

358

If your business is in your home, set parameters on the telephone hours. If your voice mail notes that business hours are from 9:00 A.M. to 6:00 P.M., Monday through Friday, your clients will quickly learn to call during those hours if they want to reach you.

359

Don't give anyone your cellular phone number. Keep the phone with you for safety reasons only or to make outgoing calls when you're en route somewhere.

Keep It Short

360

Keep a digital clock next to the phone, and watch the minutes flash away. It'll help you keep conversations brief.

361

Announce your time constraints at the beginning of the conversation. Say, "I only have five minutes. I'm on a deadline," followed by "How can I help you?" This politely directs the caller to get right down to business and keeps unnecessary chitchat to a minimum.

"I field hundreds of phone calls every week. I have to keep moving along; I don't have the time to indulge in a lot of social graces with each call. So I help the caller get to the point right away. I say, 'Let's park this truck in the garage . . . whaddya want?' Or I say, 'The meter's running . . . whaddya need?' It works every time."

Arnot Walker, Press Secretary to Peter Jennings, newscaster

Hang Up

362

End a conversation by saying that your spouse is waiting. This excuse packs a powerful punch. Rarely will you find a caller that'll keep talking with the vision of a foot-tapping spouse standing nearby.

363

If you're ready to hang up, say so. "I need to hang up now, but before I do, I want to thank you for calling. It's been great talking to you."

364

Develop stock phrases to use to get off the phone, such as:
 "I'm in the middle of a meeting, so I can't talk now."
 "I'm on my way out the door."
 "I'm late for an appointment/meeting."
 "This call is costing you money. I'd better let
  you go."

365

If all else fails, "accidentally" hang up. Later blame it on faulty phone equipment.

If They Want to Talk to You, They'll Call Back

366

If you want some temporary peace and quiet, unplug the phone.

367

If the person you're talking to is constantly interrupting the conversation to take incoming calls on another line or from call waiting, end the conversation. Ask the other party to call back when they're not so busy.

368

Never answer the telephone if you have someone else in your office or if you're entertaining company at home. It's rude.

369

It's enough to juggle phone calls all day at work; why do it at home? Get rid of call waiting at home.

370

Get rid of your answering machine at home. Why come home from church only to field phone calls that you "have" to return?

371

Don't answer the phone while you're eating. It's bad for your digestion.

372

Most of the time, answering the phone is a reflex action, born of habit and fueled by curiosity. The automatic need to know (who's calling and why) must be curbed before you can break the habit. Quit assuming that every time the phone rings, it's an important call. Half the time, it isn't. Let the machine get it.

Learn to live by the Telephone Golden Rule: Just because the telephone rings doesn't mean you have to answer it; just because someone calls you doesn't mean you have to talk to them.

Think About Errands Before You Do Them

373

When you think of an errand that needs to be done, note it on an "errands list." Unless it can't wait for some reason, hold off running that errand until you have other things to do in that part of town.

374

Keep your list of errands with you. When you're out and about you might find that you can dash into a store and do an errand without any real inconvenience.

375

Consolidate your errands by location. It's best if you can find a shopping area where you can do everything from laundry to grocery shopping.

376

Think before you run all over town to save money. Unless the savings are significant, any money you save will be offset by the time and trouble it takes to save it.

377

Reduce your errand trips by changing your buying patterns. Save trips to the post office by buying an inexpensive scale and stamps in bulk. If you're always picking up sodas or bottled water at the store, buy it by the case.

378

Instead of shopping and doing errands on the way home from work or on weekends when the stores are the most crowded, try to patronize stores that are open early in the morning or late at night during the week. An hour here and twenty minutes there adds up to more time for yourself this Saturday.

379

If you must spend part of your weekend doing errands, schedule a limited block of time (8:30 to 11:00 on Saturday morning, for example). Use the rest of the day to be productive or have fun.

380

Make a deal with your partner to alternate duties. You take care of the children one Saturday, your spouse does it the next. On your free day you can breeze through your errands and still have time left over for yourself.

381

Divide errands up among family members. If they're not old enough to drive and handle the assignment on their own, take them with you and let them find some of the items on your list while you get the rest.

382

Don't run to the store for just one item unless you absolutely have to. Wait until you have to pick up several things. Don't put only one garment in the dry cleaners, don't run to the drugstore just to pick up a magazine and don't go to the copy shop just to copy one piece of paper.

383

As soon as you've finished with a library book or videotape, put it on the table by the door so when you leave you can take it with you and drop it in the quick return slot.

384

Put a tote bag in your car for dry cleaning. As you accumulate clothes that need to be dry-cleaned, toss them into the bag in the car. The next time you pass the dry cleaners, drop them off.

Eliminate Errands Altogether

385

Get as many things as possible delivered to you. You may think you can't afford the extra service, but remember what it costs to run around shopping and completing errands. Along with the time, you save on gas and parking. Sometimes delivery really is the better deal.

386

Try swapping some of your errands with neighbors. Maybe you can pick up her dry cleaning (you're going anyway), and she can pick up stamps for you while she's at the post office.

387

Errand services can do everything for you, from picking up your cleaning to purchasing gifts and doing your grocery shopping. If you don't have time to do it yourself, hire someone. If you're on a budget, a senior citizen or a teenager might be able to lend a hand for a reasonable amount of money.

Reduce Trips to the Grocery Store

388

Keep a grocery list in the kitchen and note items that you need when they run low but *before* you run out. You'll always have what you need when you need it.

389

Go to the store once rather than several times a week. Running to pick something up after work only increases your stress level and wastes time since that's when the store is likely to be the most crowded.

390

Plan your menu for the upcoming week. Check to make sure you have all the necessary ingredients in stock. Don't wait until six on Tuesday night to make an irritating last-minute run to the store to pick up just one item for the meat loaf.

391

Organize your shopping list according to location. List all the produce together, the meat, the soups, and so on. You'll avoid wandering back and forth at the store looking for things.

Use Kitchen Shortcuts

392

Take time on Saturday or Sunday to plan your menu for the entire week.

393

Work out a week's worth of recipes that can be made in twenty minutes or less. Keep ingredients on hand for those meals. When you get home late or are just too tired to cook, toss together one of these quick meals.

394

If you haven't planned your menu for the week, at least make it a point to decide early in the day what you'll have that evening. Don't wait until you're exhausted at five to try to figure it out.

"Ask your child what he wants for dinner only if he's buying."
Fran Lebowitz, Author, Social Studies

395

You don't have to constantly vary your dinner menus. If you like the same five or ten dishes, stick to those dishes on a rotating basis until you get sick of them.

396

Do small things in advance. Wash salad fixings and store them in food storage bags or containers. Brown ground meat, cut up onions and other "choppables" that you'll be using in the next few days. Hard-boil some eggs. Clean and cut carrot and celery sticks. You'll have healthy snacks to grab or food that's ready to go into a meal later in the week.

397

Try freezing food in small servings. They're easier to defrost and can be used for a single meal or snack. Defrost more servings for a meal for several people.

398

Wrap and date items that go into the freezer. Put each new item in the *back* of the freezer, and move everything else forward.

399

Buy paper cups and plates. You'll be amazed at the difference in dish duty even if all you do is drink your coffee, milk, water, soda and other beverages out of paper cups instead of washable cups and glasses.

400

Shop once or twice a month in bulk and prepare and freeze meals ahead. Make it a family affair. One person can do the shopping, another does the washing, another the chopping, and another cooks and freezes the food. Everyone helps clean up the mess. The result is several days of home-cooked meals that can be put on the table at the end of a hectic day with little or no effort.

401

If you're cooking or baking, double up and freeze one portion to eat later. It's just as easy to cook two meat loaves as one, and it's not extra work to make a double batch of spaghetti sauce. Freeze the second portion, and it'll give you an evening when all you need to do for the main dish is thaw it and heat it up.

402

It costs a bit more, but you can save time by purchasing prepared items at the grocery store. Bags of precut and washed lettuce and vegetables can make salad preparation a five-minute rather than a fifteen-minute task. Chicken that's been precut for stir-fry reduces the thirty to forty minutes spent deboning and chopping to less than one minute of tossing of the pieces into the pan.

403

Dig that Crock-Pot out of the back of the cabinet and get up twenty minutes early tomorrow to put a meal together in the pot. Set it on low, and when you get home from work, dinner will be ready.

404

Get organized before you cook. Gather all the ingredients and the pots and pans you'll be using. Don't wait until you get in the middle of cooking something to discover that you don't have the next ingredient.

405

Turn on your exhaust fan when you cook. You'll save grease buildup on appliances and surfaces close to the stove.

406

Cook in an extra large container so it doesn't boil over and require extra time to clean up the stove or oven.

407

Use disposable roasting pans for those once-in-a-while meals— like the turkey during the holidays. After a big dinner, the last thing you want to do is tackle the challenges of a greasy roasting pan.

408

To cut down on scrubbing, line the bottoms of your baking dishes and pans with aluminum foil. The foil catches grease and other messes that would otherwise bake onto the dish.

409

Cooking time allows time for spot five-minute jobs. While you're waiting for something to boil, you can wipe a refrigerator shelf or two, wash the knife and fork organizer and wipe out a drawer. Tackle the kitchen with regular five-minute jobs, and you'll be able to avoid devoting an entire day to it before your mother-in-law arrives.

410

If you have a hard time getting everything on the table at the same time, set a timer for ten minutes before the main dish is to be done. Use that ten minutes for any last-minute things, like warming the biscuits or adding tomatoes to the salad.

411

Put a lazy Susan in the middle of your table to hold sugar, salt, pepper and other condiments. This makes everything instantly accessible, eliminating requests to "please pass" this or that across the table.

412

Clean up before you sit down. Clean off the counters and put pots and pans in the sink to soak before you sit down to eat.

413

To save steps, use a dishpan or litter pan to "bus" dishes from the dining room to the kitchen rather than carrying only one or two items at a time.

414

Alternate cooking duties with your spouse. You cook one week and she cooks the next.

415

If your husband is reluctant to cook, get him hooked on the food processor. Move the barbecue grill to a safe place close to the door so he can cook out all year long.

416

Tell the children that they can start getting dinner ready before you get home. A fourteen-year-old doesn't need you standing there in order to get a salad washed and tossed.

417

Delegate kitchen cleanup to family members. To reduce the time spent fussing and arguing over cleaning up the kitchen after dinner, make a rule that the kitchen has to be completely cleaned up within forty-five minutes after the last person has left the table.

418

If you tend to rely on take-out food for meals, save yourself a step by keeping copies of the menus at work. You can call the order in and pick it up on the way home. This eliminates having to go back out once you get home.

419

Try to make it a habit (twice a month, for example) to order in or eat out. Every time you do this you'll save yourself at least one or two hours in the kitchen cooking and cleaning. At a savings of two hours, if you only do it twice a month, by the end of the year you'll have saved almost *two full days* in the kitchen!

420

Don't go to the market when you're hungry. You'll overspend and buy things you have no business eating in the first place.

421

Stick to the items on your list. If you have to take children with you, teach them early on that you only purchase what is on the list.

422

Don't go overboard with coupons. It takes time to clip, organize and redeem them. Make sure all that time is worth the money you save. And don't buy things that you wouldn't normally buy just because you have a coupon.

423

Buying items in bulk can save money, but don't do it unless you have pest-free storage space for the extras. Beware of buying more than you'd ever realistically use. The money you saved will then be lost when things go bad.

424

When you bring groceries home, take a few minutes to wash, precut and package some of the vegetables you'll be using in the next few days. You'll be glad for the time it'll save during the upcoming week.

Cut Your Housework off at the Door

"Life is 5 percent joy, 5 percent grief, and 90 percent maintenance."

Harriet Schechter, Author of More Time for Sex

425

Dirt comes in the door. Cut down on the dirt that comes into the house by having a good mat outside and inside all doors.

426

Get in the habit of removing your shoes when you're in the house; the floors will stay cleaner longer.

427

If you don't have a mudroom, improvise. Set up a laundry basket near the door for hats, mittens, snowsuits, etc. The vented sides let things dry out. Put a thick rug or large mat under the basket to catch any moisture. Add a second mat to hold wet or muddy shoes and boots.

428

Pay attention to high-traffic "pathways" in your house. Wherever you can, put washable rugs down in those areas. Rugs help prevent ground-in dirt and stop wear and tear on your floor coverings.

429

Just as dirt comes in the door, dust comes in the windows. The more you keep your windows closed, the less dust you'll have.

430

Try to avoid storing things in open, high places where dust and dirt collect.

"I only break down and dust my curio cabinet when company is coming. There, I said it, and I don't care who knows it."
Julie McNeary, Columnist, The Californian

431

Make sure you check your air filters regularly. A dirty filter eventually circulates that dirt through your house.

432

If your pet sleeps on your bed at night, put a sheet over the top of the bed. In the morning, remove it and shake it out. Your bed will stay cleaner longer.

433

Install a paper towel rack in the bathroom. Teach your family to use them for drying hands and face (saving on towels and laundry) and before they toss the paper towel, tell them to give the counter a quick wipe.

434

Keep disposable cups in the bathroom to insure germ-free hygiene and to cut down on washing bathroom cups and glasses.

435

Replace bar soap at your sinks with soap in a pump dispenser. There's less waste, and the sink area stays cleaner without the residue that bar soap leaves.

436

To help keep mildew at bay in the bathroom, open the window when you shower.

437

To help keep soap scum under control, keep a squeegee in the shower so that everyone can give the walls a quick wipe after each shower.

438

Make it a habit to take a few minutes and clean up as you go along, from cleaning up as you cook to cleaning paint brushes and tools as soon as you're done with them. Keeping on top of things all along means any final mess will be minor.

439

Avoid cleaning up surprise messes and stains by setting limits on how far food and drinks can travel in the house. Once food and drinks start moving from place to place there's a good chance they will get spilled on furniture and carpets. Make a rule that food stays in the kitchen, dining room and family room and goes nowhere else in the house.

440

Make sure you have degreasers and stain removers on hand to quickly treat a spill or spot as soon as it happens. Treating things immediately can remove the stain and spare you lots of effort later on.

Develop Good Cleaning Habits

441

Keep cleaning materials near areas that need regular cleanup. For example, keep at least a sponge, cleanser, glass cleaner and paper towels in the bathrooms. Keep a whisk broom and dustpan near the kitty litter box.

442

Buy some inexpensive washcloths to use as cleaning rags. Use them for mini-towels in the kitchen too. They make great hand wipers and can be better than paper towels for mopping up unexpected spills or polishing the chrome on sink fixtures.

443

When towels or flannel pajamas are worn out, cut them up into cleaning rags. Periodically toss them into the washer and you'll always have a great supply of cleaning rags.

444

If you move from room to room with cleaning supplies, put them all in a handy carryall caddy or bucket so you can carry them all at once.

445

When you clean, carry a giant trash bag with you so you can collect trash as you go.

446

Always clean from the top down, then vacuum or mop your way out of the room.

447

Seventy-five percent of cleaning is chemical, so don't spend so much time and energy scrubbing. Brush off the loose dirt, then soak the item and clean.

448

When you clean the metal filter above your stove, don't waste time scrubbing it. Put it in your dishwasher instead.

449

Put your kitchen sponges in the dishwasher with the dirty dishes. The high heat dry setting will kill any bacteria on the sponge.

450

To make quick work of cleaning out a coffee (or tea) carafe or a thermos, put a capful of bleach inside and fill it with water. Wait a few minutes and rinse. The item will sparkle.

451

Never mop the floor with just one bucket or one sink full of soapy water. Always have one bucket of soapy water; but before you dip the mop back into it, rinse the mop out in clear water. You'll do a better job cleaning the floor because you won't be re-using dirty mop water.

452

If you hate cleaning the bathrooms, start there. Do the worst first, and the rest of your housework day will be easier.

453

Make everyone in the family give the tub a quick cleanup as they get out of it. It'll be ready for the next person and will be easier to clean thoroughly on cleaning day.

454

Use a long-handled stiff brush to clean the tub instead of a rag or sponge. It cleans better, and you won't have to bend as much.

455

Make sure you always have a backup supply of vacuum cleaner bags as well as a spare belt. You won't have to quit in the middle of vacuuming just because the bag is full or a belt breaks.

"Never purchase a tool to clean behind radiators, because you won't have an excuse not to clean there."
Charlotte Johnston, Family Circle *magazine*

456

Keep a vacuum cleaner on each floor of your house so you don't have to haul one up and down the stairs. Have a heavy-duty extension cord for each vacuum so you don't have to constantly plug and unplug it as you go from room to room.

457

Vacuum frequently. It prolongs the life of your carpet and helps keep dirt from turning into a stain.

458

Vacuum your blinds at least once a month, and you won't have to worry about taking them down for a major cleaning once a year.

459

If you have pets, don't use a rag to dust; use the vacuum. You'll have better control over the hair and dander.

460

If your living room is a museum (you only use it twice a year when company comes), don't waste time cleaning it all the time. Just clean it now and then, or right before company is due.

461

Accept a little less spit and polish so long as the basics are taken care of and the place is organized.

"Forget the old cliché to the effect that anything worth doing is worth doing well. This isn't true. When you're going at a high lope, a fast swipe at the sink is a lot better than no swipe at all."

Peg Bracken, Author, The I Hate to Housekeep Book

462

Stop demanding that the place be perfectly clean and spotless and don't clean anything that isn't dirty. It'll get dirty soon enough. Then you can clean it.

Keep on Top of the Laundry

463

Don't put your clothes in the laundry unless they're dirty. Wear them again if they're still perfectly clean.

464

Don't automatically wash towels after only one use. Towels really can be used more than once before they hit the hamper.

465

Stop changing your sheets every week if it isn't necessary. Change them only when they need to be changed.

466

Most people do the laundry because the supply of clean underwear is running low. Make sure everyone's supply of undies is plentiful, and you can cut back on frequent underwear-related washings.

467

Put three bins in the laundry area, marked *whites*, *darks* and *colors*. Instruct family members to bring their own dirty clothes to the laundry and sort them into the appropriate bins.

468

Put a shelf in the laundry room with a basket for each member of the family. When clothes come out of the dryer, simply sort them into the appropriate basket and have each family member retrieve, fold and put away their own clothes.

469

Keep some sewing supplies near the laundry so when you spot a loose button or small rip you can make a quick repair.

470

Keep a cigar box or similar container in the laundry room to collect items that you pull out of pockets.

471

Hang a bulletin board in the laundry area to post spot removal information or special care instructions for various items of clothing.

472

Put a trash can in the laundry area for any empty soap containers, dryer lint, used fabric softener sheets or other trash that accumulates.

473

If you have several family members, get each of them a mesh bag with their name on it for their dirty underwear. Toss the bags into the washer and dryer. You'll eliminate sorting altogether.

474

Teach your kids how to do laundry as soon as they're big enough. If you have three kids and they each only do one load per week, that's three loads of wash that you don't have to do.

475

Have everybody in the house toss their whites into the washing machine every day. When it's full, run a load.

476

Keep a spot remover stick in everyone's bedroom and bathroom so they can treat spots on their clothes before they toss them into the hamper.

477

Have a clothes hamper in each bedroom to make it easy for everyone to pick up their dirty clothes.

478

Refuse to wash clothes that you have to personally hunt for and gather up. If your kids don't have their dirty clothes in the hampers, let it go. The next time your teenager suddenly needs a particular blouse and it's dirty, she'll have a lesson in laundry instead of a clean blouse.

479

If you're always losing socks, buy socks in one style and one color. Then when one is lost, the odd mate can be tossed in with the others, and you'll replace complete pairs less frequently.

480

Use the same colored towels and linens throughout the house; it makes it easier to restock. You won't have to wait until the blue sheets for the blue room are washed; you can use the plain white ones that are already in the linen closet.

481

Don't let your clothing sit in the washer after the machine has stopped. Take the clothes out immediately and shake out each item as you put it into the dryer. Remove the clothes from the dryer as soon as they're dry. You'll reduce wrinkles and ironing time.

482

You can wash most delicate items in the machine if you put them in a lingerie bag and set the washer on a gentle, cold water cycle.

483

Don't cram your washer and dryer to the brim. There should be room for the clothes to move around. They'll come out cleaner and drier if the machine isn't jam-packed.

484

If your load of clothes is taking too long to dry, add a couple of dry, clean towels. It speeds the drying process.

485

Instead of doing five loads of laundry on Saturday, try doing one load each day. You'll buy yourself a glorious laundry-free Saturday as a result.

486

To make short work of an excess amount of laundry, take it all to a laundromat. You can wash and dry all your loads at once and be done with it in a fraction of the time it would take to do it at home, one load at a time.

487

Send some of your laundry to the professional laundry. Count how many hours you spend each week ironing and multiply that by fifty-two, then double that figure because it's so incredibly tedious. Send it out. It's worth every penny.

488

If you take your laundry to a Laundromat, throw quarters into a cup throughout the week. When you're ready to do the laundry you won't have to scrounge for change.

489

If you use a Laundromat, try to go during off-hours so you won't have to wait for a machine.

Get Some Help

490

Between cleaning, laundry, ironing and cleaning the kitchen, it's easy to spend twelve hours per week on housework. By the end of the year, that adds up to 624 unrewarding hours devoted to housework. Hire someone else to do at least some of the housework for you.

491

If you can't afford a housekeeper every week, try for twice a month. That might be all you need to get the scrubbing chores done; the rest of the time you can keep up with light maintenance.

492

Be available to spend time training people, whether it's your kids or a housekeeper, so they know how you like to have things done. Review how they did it, and gently point out what needs to be done better. Eventually, everything will get done—and some of it will meet your standards.

493

Hire somebody, even a teenager, to do your yard work once a month. They can weed, rake, trim and do other extra jobs that need to be done outside.

494

To lighten your housework load, consider paying your baby-sitter a bit extra to do some light housework for you.

495

Trade chores with a friend. If she likes cleaning out cupboards, and you like stripping and waxing floors, let her do your cupboards, and you do her floors.

496

Make sure everyone helps out with the housework. Use the Golden Rule of Housework: Except for babies in diapers, no one is too young or too male to help with the housework.

497

If you don't know how to start delegating chores, make a detailed list of exactly everything you do. Lighten your load by giving away some of the chores to your spouse and children.

498

Make a housework notebook. Have one page for each room and make a specific list of exactly what should be done in that room. Wipe windowsill. Clean sink and counter. Scrub tub. Clean toilet inside and out. Clean mirror and polish chrome. Sweep and mop floor. Divide up the chores among family members so they know exactly what's expected. Or, let your housekeeper use your list so she knows just what to do in each room.

499

If your family has never done anything to help out with the housework, start slowly. Give everybody three things to do every day and four or five things to do on Saturday.

500

Put aside your worries about infringing on others' time. Other people's time may be valuable, but so is yours. Don't be afraid to ask for, and expect, help.

"If someone refuses to do a certain chore because it is beneath their status, I have to wonder how this person values the person they expect to do the job."
    Toni Pighetti, Author, Stop the Vacuum! I Want to Get Off

---

501

Let family members know what's expected of them in advance. If you want your teenager to do three loads of laundry on Saturday, don't wait until Saturday morning to issue the order.

502

Use a chore list and calendar. Write down who is supposed to do what for at least a week at a time. Post it for everyone to see. This way you can bypass that ever popular "Nope, it's not my turn to load the dishwasher (or feed the pets, or whatever)."

503

Rotate the chore list so that everybody gets a turn at each chore. You can rotate toilet cleaning responsibilities or use it as a punishment. The army is very successful at using latrine duty to get the troops to be more cooperative.

504

You can pay your kids to do things if you must (Erma Bombeck claimed she paid her kids to breathe). But when they're twenty-one years old who's going to pay them to pick up and wash their dirty underwear?

505

Make a rule that certain chores—whether it's taking out the trash, loading the dishwasher or making the bed—have to be done every day.

506

Don't be a sap and let one person get off the chore hook. If you do, before you know it you'll have a mutiny on your hands, and everybody will be jumping off the housework ship.

507

Many hands make light work. Don't make one family member help out with the housework more than other members. Since everyone enjoys the benefits of a well-run, clean household, each person should contribute to its maintenance.

508

It takes time to train children to do chores. But don't give in to whining, procrastinating or poorly done work. Once they know you mean business, things will improve and you'll have less work to do yourself.

509

Expect to explain not only how, but why things are done a particular way. Training time with children can be lengthy but ultimately rewarding, so don't give up.

510

Give a deadline for chore completion, and use a timer to enforce it. "You have forty-five minutes to pick up everything in your room, make your bed and empty the kitchen trash."

511

Give small children short deadlines—even if it's only five minutes (to put their coat and boots away, for example). Without deadlines, they'll dawdle.

512

The younger the child, the more the chore needs to be broken down. Don't say "Clean up this mess." Instead, say "Pick up all your toys and put them in your room. Hang up your coat. Put your schoolbooks on the table by the door. Put the uneaten popcorn in the trash and put the bowl in the dishwasher."

513

Don't wait until your child's room is out of control before you deal with it. Have daily five-minute reviews and insist that the child clean up the room in small, manageable, child-size tasks (assigned by you).

514

Make your children completely responsible for their bedroom plus two other daily chores. It sounds less daunting when you say "your room plus two things" than if you say "You have chores to do today."

515

Keep an eye out for sabotage. The person who cleans the bathroom once and does a pathetic job of it is likely doing it poorly on purpose. Give them the opportunity to do it over. Eventually they'll get the message that sabotage tactics don't work.

516

Don't let kids play until the last minute. Ask them to stop at least ten minutes early to pick up their toys and put them away.

517

Turn chore time into talk time. Make dinner together, fold clothes together, rake leaves and pull weeds, and run errands together. Visit with each other as you work.

518

For especially big jobs, start everybody early and promise a reward (you'll go out for ice cream) and a stopping point if everyone cooperates. Try to stop when everyone has time left for themselves. No one likes devoting their entire weekend to chores.

519

Make sure you have some consequences in mind if, in spite of your directions, the chores don't get done by your loved ones. Then mete out those consequences. Stick to your guns.

520

If your husband says he doesn't have to do housework because he does yard work, swap with him. Yard work usually takes about a tenth of the time housework does. Keep the swap up as long as you can; eventually he might agree to a sensible compromise where he helps out inside the house a bit, as well as taking care of the outside.

521

If your husband doesn't know how to iron his own shirts, teach him. If he balks, toss them in the car and give him the address of the nearest professional laundry. He can drop them off, pick them up, and pay for them himself.

522

Don't automatically pick up after your children and spouse. Give them the opportunity to grow into better human beings by picking up after themselves.

523

Use positive reinforcement. Compliment completed tasks and issue positive reminders. Spouses never tire of hearing the words "thank you." Children especially appreciate being praised in front of others.

524

Be prepared to reduce your expectations. A poorly made bed is not as good as a well-made one, but it's better than an unmade bed. Remember, practice makes perfect.

525

Resist the urge to do it yourself so it can be done exactly "right." Most housework doesn't have to be done exactly right. It just needs to be done.

"If you are doing most of the (house) work, you've got the problem. They do not. As it now stands, they allow and expect you to continue indefinitely. If you think that they will voluntarily take over some of your responsibilities, be prepared for a disappointment."

Toni Pighetti, Author, Stop the Vacuum! I Want to Get Off

526

Don't get obsessed with how something is done. If a family member has a different way of doing the laundry, focus on the results rather than the methods. If the laundry comes out clean and is folded and hung up with a minimum of wrinkles, who cares how it was done? The point is, it's done.

527

Don't let anyone claim sainthood for helping out. Since the people who routinely do the work have never been able to profess sainthood, other family members who pitch in shouldn't be elevated to the status of a saint either. A simple thank-you should suffice, and you should expect more of the same help on a regular basis. Period.

528

If you feel like you've become an unappreciated slave, maybe it's true. Go on strike. Don't do housework, the laundry or cooking. Don't go to the store. Forget the errands. Do what everybody else does. Sit around and wait for somebody else to do it all. A strike might get everyone to the chore-negotiating table.

Have a Little Fun

529

Match your housework to your energy level. If you are your peppiest at night, do it then.

530

Turn the TV off when you clean—the temptation to stop and watch can turn a few hours of work into an all-day affair. Play some upbeat music instead. You can sing and dance your way through the dusting and mopping.

531

Where is it written that you always have to clean house on the weekend? This weekend, let it go. Do something fun instead.

Make Time to Read

"I think a perfect way to spend a lunch hour at work is to read. I'd rather curl up with a good book for an hour than eat."

Glenda Winders, Editorial Manager, Copley News Service

532

Be selective about what you read. Don't feel obligated to read something just because you always have or because someone passed it along to you (such as an article that someone mailed to you). If it isn't something you need or want to read, get rid of it.

533

Evaluate your subscription list regularly and let some of your subscriptions lapse. If you order a new subscription, don't renew an old one.

534

Don't feel obligated to read everything you receive. Some of it isn't worth your time. Trash or recycle it.

535

Before you read anything, check the table of contents. Then clip only what's worth reading, and throw the rest of the periodical away.

536

Not everything needs to be read in depth. If something only needs to be scanned, don't waste time getting involved in it.

537

Don't bother finishing an article you've started reading if it turns out to be boring or irrelevant. Chuck it, and save yourself some time.

538

If you spend time perusing several publications looking for articles on a particular topic of interest, consider hiring a clipping service instead. They'll send you just the articles you need.

539

Always carry reading materials with you. You can catch up on your reading during unexpected moments of waiting or downtime.

540

Break down your reading. If you can't read an entire book, and don't know when you'll ever have the time, schedule enough time to read two chapters each week, and in six weeks or so, you'll have finished the book.

541

Find a quiet place to read. Turn off the TV and telephone. You'll be able to read more and get more out of it.

542

Don't buy more books and publications if you already have a stack waiting for you back at the office or at home that you still haven't read.

543

If you really want more time to read a book, stop reading magazines and newspapers.

544

Don't read when you go to bed if you always fall asleep ten minutes later. Instead, set aside a half hour or so, before you go to bed, to read. You'll get more out of it.

545

If you don't have time to read anything else in a day, at least make it a habit to take a few minutes and read something motivational, inspirational or humorous. A prayer, an affirmation or a cartoon can lift your day.

Finding Time for You and Yours

Put People in Their Place

546

Evaluate the place people hold in your life. Not everyone is equally important. Friendships and relationships should be selected with great care. When they're treated with consideration and respect, they can last a lifetime. If you find yourself neglecting people who matter to you, perhaps you need to reevaluate your priorities. Decide who means the most to you and devote your prime time to them.

547

When a relationship starts to develop problems, deal with those issues openly and immediately. It'll save you time, anxiety and energy down the road.

548

Relationships don't necessarily last a lifetime. Occasionally you have to make the decision to move on, letting some associations, friendships and relationships go in the process. If a relationship has become a drain, a strain or just a plain old pain, it may be time to let it go.

Spend Time With Your Family

549

Don't let your kids sign up for so many activities that they're never at home. Extracurricular activities should not take the place of family time all the time.

550

Don't sign up for more overtime than you have to. More time with the family is worth a lot more than money.

551

Bring back the daily dinner hour. Establish a consistent dinner time and insist that everyone be there. Don't commit yourself or your children to activities that conflict with that hour. During dinner, don't answer the telephone and turn off the television.

552

Make Sunday dinner a regular event for the family. Invite a friend or relative over at least once each month to join you. And yes, the football game gets turned off during dinner.

553

Turn a table into a work center for the whole family. While your children do their homework, sit with them and do yours. Pay bills, flip through catalogs, sort coupons, and organize tomorrow's To Do list.

554

Beware of the vast amounts of time family members fritter away on the phone. Limit the amount of time a teen spends on the phone. Set limits on Internet time as well. Spend less time on the phone and more time together.

555

Turn one night every week into game night. Get the family together with a tub of popcorn to play cards and board games. Keep score, and once a month designate a game champion for the month.

556

Make plans for the entire family to take a special outing together. Do this once a month, and put it on the calendar in advance.

557

Establish a meaningful "must attend" family tradition. It can be as silly as a goofy dinner every year on April Fools' Day or as significant as special religious observances that the family always celebrates together. Remind everyone of the date in advance, and turn the time spent together into lifelong memories.

558

Don't do things *for* your children. Do things *with* them. Make Saturday mornings the time for family chores. Everyone can pitch in to do housework, yard work, shopping and errands. Cook and bake together, have everyone clean their rooms or rake leaves together. The chores will get done sooner and you'll have spent time together.

559

Worship together. Don't accept excuses (too tired, have something else to do, etc.). Stop off for a family meal at a restaurant after services. You'll spend quality time together *and* establish a family tradition.

"Time with my family can be hard to come by. So I carve out a week's vacation each year to spend with my two boys. No one else is ever invited along. We go canoeing, camping, sailing; each trip is different. No one knows exactly where we are, so I can't be reached by phone. I begin planning the trip six to eight months in advance. The boys tend to get more excited as we get closer to our time together; it becomes a major event that we all look forward to. After the trip, we hang pictures of our adventures on the wall, and delight in telling and retelling stories about our experiences together. Each of these vacations has added another building block to our relationship. The trips give us time to simply know and enjoy each other, and create memories that hopefully will live on long after me."

Dr. Ronald D. Hart, Oncologist specializing in breast cancer

560

Honor your plans. Don't change your mind or beg off at the last minute. Your family will know that you don't consider them important enough to be a priority in your life.

Put Romance in Your Life

"Money, success, and power have their charms, but to most women, a life without love is an incomplete one."

Ruth Klein, Author, Where Did the Time Go?

561

Prioritize romance. If you don't think of it as a priority, you'll never get around to it.

562

Stop working nights and weekends. If you can't do that, at least set aside Sundays or two weeknights when you absolutely do not touch work.

"I make it a point to plan the upcoming weekend at the beginning of my week. If necessary, I'll work longer during the week so that I can have my weekend clear. Saturday is my free day. I schedule dates, but I also try to reserve some time to make spontaneous plans. When I take work home, I leave it until Sunday night before I look at it. I need the rest of my weekend clear to be just me—without my work."
Jennifer Sifton, Senior Vice-President and Group Manager,
Edelman Public Relations Worldwide

563

Share the household chores. If only one person is responsible for all of the chores and child care, he or she will always be too pooped for romance. Pitch in, and you'll both have more time for regular romantic rewards.

564

Learn to say no to the kids. You don't have to give in to every demand on your time. Save some time for your spouse.

565

Don't let your kids stay up half the night. Put them on a bedtime schedule and stick to it. You should have a few quiet hours to yourselves every night.

566

Teach your child to respect your quiet time. Buy a bagful of dollar items and give a small child a timer. Set the timer for an allotted "quiet time" and promise the child a gift from the bag if they don't bother you until the timer goes off.

567

If necessary, put a lock on your bedroom door. Children do not need to watch television, play games or get dressed in their parents' bedroom, and they should be taught to knock before entering. Parents need that room for rest, recuperation and romance.

568

Make it a point to schedule one night each week when you go to bed early and one morning on the weekend when you sleep in late.

569

Cook a special meal for no particular reason. Or go out to dinner at a fine restaurant on the spur of the moment. You have to eat anyway, why not turn it into a romantic event?

570

Plan a long morning together now and then. Once a month have someone watch your kids while you enjoy a late morning and breakfast out, followed by a walk in the park.

571

Schedule a date together for a lingering lunch at least once a month.

572

Once in a blue moon, throw caution to the wind. Get to work a bit later than usual or take an extra long lunch hour. Spend that bit of extra time romantically. You'll feel like a million bucks when you do.

573

Take a day off and have your spouse do the same. Spend the time together doing something relaxing or romantic.

574

Turn one night into "date" night. Get the kids in bed, early. Turn off the television and don't answer the phone. Just spend time with each other.

575

Schedule a night out on a regular basis. Get out a least once a month. Twice a month is better, and once a week is ideal. Trade baby-sitting services with a friend, if sitting fees are a problem. Go out to dinner, to the movies or just look at the stars.

576

Schedule a long weekend away alone at least once every three months. Alternate who does the planning. You plan one and your partner plans the next. This takes the burden of all the planning off one person and increases the chance that each person will enjoy the date thoroughly, especially when it's their turn to plan.

577

Establish a small daily tradition. Get up earlier than your spouse and deliver the first cup of coffee to the bedroom. Bring a single flower home every Friday. Little things mean a lot.

578

Make it a point every day to say something loving and include a sincere hug. Like time, bits and pieces of romance can add up over the long haul and make a big difference in your life.

Get Out and Meet People

579

If you tend to sit home when you know you should be out trying to meet people, schedule something specific to do for the next four Saturday nights. Get a friend to go with you if you can.

580

If you never have time to go out and meet new people because you work so much, stop working so much.

581

If you want to develop a social life but don't know where to start, begin by joining a club, a gym or a charitable organization. Sign up for an athletic group activity. Take a class. Go to church. You'll meet all kinds of people.

582

Tell the people you know that you'd like to know more people.

583

Be neighborly. Make it a point to take a few minutes to say hello to your neighbors at least once a week. Offer your help with little things. Be generous with your friendliness. Enthusiastically welcome new neighbors. Take the initiative to be a good neighbor and you'll find yourself with good neighbors that you can count on.

Set Aside Regular Time for Friends

"Don't waste time trying to be your own best friend; you can't pat yourself on the back, and it's unsatisfying to cry on your own shoulder. Find a real friend instead."
                    Charlotte Johnston, Family Circle *magazine*

584

Regardless of how busy you are, make time for your friends. It's time well spent.

585

To make sure you find time for friends throughout the year, order theater or concert tickets as soon as they become available. Mark the dates on your calendar and ask friends in advance to go with you.

586

If you never have time to get together with a friend, schedule an activity and a visit. Go shopping together or exercise together. Do errands and go to lunch together.

587

If you don't have time to meet friends for lunch, get together for breakfast instead.

588

If you don't have time to visit friends in person, arrange to talk to them by phone for an hour or two.

Set Aside Prime Time for Yourself

589

Schedule personal time for yourself, and write that appointment down on your calendar just as you would any other. Blocks of time are best—even if it's only two hours on a Saturday morning. If you can't manage that, try to fit in a half hour, two or three times a week. Don't use the time for chores; use it to do something relaxing or fun.

590

If you're too busy to think, much less solve problems or plan ahead, schedule at least one hour a week to sit down in a quiet place to do nothing more than gather your thoughts. Better yet, schedule thirty minutes every day for creative thinking. You'll inspire yourself to greatness after a while.

591

Don't spend your time doing things for others that they should be doing for themselves. Give up being the hero or the fixer of all things. You'll never have time for yourself if you're always out solving everyone else's problems.

592

When you come in from work make it a habit to insist on fifteen minutes of quiet time by yourself as you shift from the work day to the evening schedule. The children's demands can wait while you change, hop in the shower or just spend a few minutes resting quietly in your bedroom before you hit the kitchen.

593

Don't schedule lunch dates, and don't agree to meet people after work. You can use that time as time for yourself instead.

594

If every evening seems like nothing but a round of chores, take control of the schedule by planning something pleasant to do, even if it's only a thirty-minute walk with your spouse or spending a half hour in the basement working on your hobby.

595

See if you can work four ten-hour days rather than five eight-hour days. You'll have an entire day for yourself during the week.

596

When you're feeling completely overwhelmed, take some sick days or a personal day or two. Take a day off once in a while for no particular reason. You can call it a mental health day.

597

Give yourself a break. Don't plan anything this weekend. Relax and do nothing.

Watch Less TV

"The average American watches ten years of TV in a lifetime, including two years of commercials."

TV Guide

598

Don't let television be a priority in your life. Make plans to do things, have undisturbed family time and meals, and go places. Watch TV only after all those activities are finished.

599

Don't automatically turn the television on the minute you get home. If you do, you'll eventually find yourself addicted to it—if only to the background noise. If you're really not watching it, turn it off.

600

Decide in advance what you're going to watch. Don't channel surf; it's mindless.

601

Watch only programs that are really good or that you always enjoy. Turn the television off the rest of the time. If you think a program will be good, but after the first fifteen minutes you're not interested, turn the TV off immediately.

602

Don't get addicted to soap operas. If you must watch them, select one or two, then watch two or three times a week. You won't miss anything.

603

Your undivided attention isn't always required to follow a program. Make the bed, cook dinner, dust furniture and do other chores with the TV within earshot, and you'll be surprised at how little you really miss.

604

Do something productive during commercials. In five minutes you can unload a dishwasher or change a bed.

605

Record programs you want to see on a VCR. When you watch them, fast-forward through the commercials. While it might be considered sacrilegious by some, you could even tape a football game for later. Zap through commercials and halftime, and a game could easily be seen in an hour or less rather than taking up an entire afternoon.

If you really want more time for yourself, your friends and your family, unplug the telephone, the TV and the computer.

606

Have television-free time zones. For example, don't turn the TV on during meals or on Sunday before one o'clock. Those TV-free times will give you an opportunity to tackle things you've been putting off, read a good book or spend time with friends and family.

607

If you reduce your TV viewing time by only five hours each week, you'll gain nearly eleven days a year.

Understand the Value of Your Time

"You only live once—but if you work it right, once is enough."
Joe E. Lewis

608

Ask yourself what others will say about you at your funeral. Write your own obituary. Check what's missing, and start fine-tuning your life to give it some meaning.

609

Spend time like money—carefully.

610

Vow to do less so you can take time to enjoy your life. Now. Before it's too late.

611

Know that each moment of your life, once spent, is gone forever. Live your life with that in mind, and then plan to make each moment count.

Send in Your Tip:

If you have a tip on how to save time or get organized, I'd love to hear from you. Please send your tip to me directly at the following address:

Stephanie Culp
The Organization
P.O. Box 890700
Temecula, CA 92589

(909) 506-0044
Fax: (909) 506-0024